Superhero Phonic Readers

Jumping Jade

written by Mandy Ross

illustrated by Mark Ruffle

Meet Jumping Jade.
Jumping Jade can jump as high
as a house. Or higher!

How to use Superhero Phonic Readers:

⭐ These stories are perfect for children who have learnt their letters and sounds in school. Start at level one and gradually progress through the series. Each story is a little bit longer than the last and uses more grown-up vocabulary.

⭐ Children will be able to read **Superhero Phonic Readers** for themselves. Let your child read to you, and share the excitement!

⭐ If your child finds a word difficult, help him or her to work out the sounds in the word.

⭐ Early readers can be concentrating so hard on the words that they sometimes don't fully grasp the overall meaning of what they read. The puzzle questions on pages 28 and 29 will help with this. Have fun talking about them together.

⭐ The Ladybird website **www.ladybird.com** features a wealth of information about phonics and reading.

⭐ Enjoy reading together!

Geraldine Taylor - Ladybird Educational Consultant

Educational Consultant: Geraldine Taylor
Phonics Consultant: Marj Newbury

A catalogue record for this book is available from the British Library

Published by Ladybird Books Ltd
80 Strand, London, WC2R 0RL
A Penguin Company

2 4 6 8 10 9 7 5 3 1
© LADYBIRD BOOKS LTD MMIX
LADYBIRD and the device of a Ladybird are trademarks of Ladybird Books Ltd

ISBN: 978-1-40930-160-8

Printed in Italy

Jumping Jade likes to jump from
roof to roof.

Do not do this at home, readers.

One day, Jumping Jade is jumping from roof to roof when she hears… nee-naw, nee-naw!

Jumping Jade can see police cars speeding to…

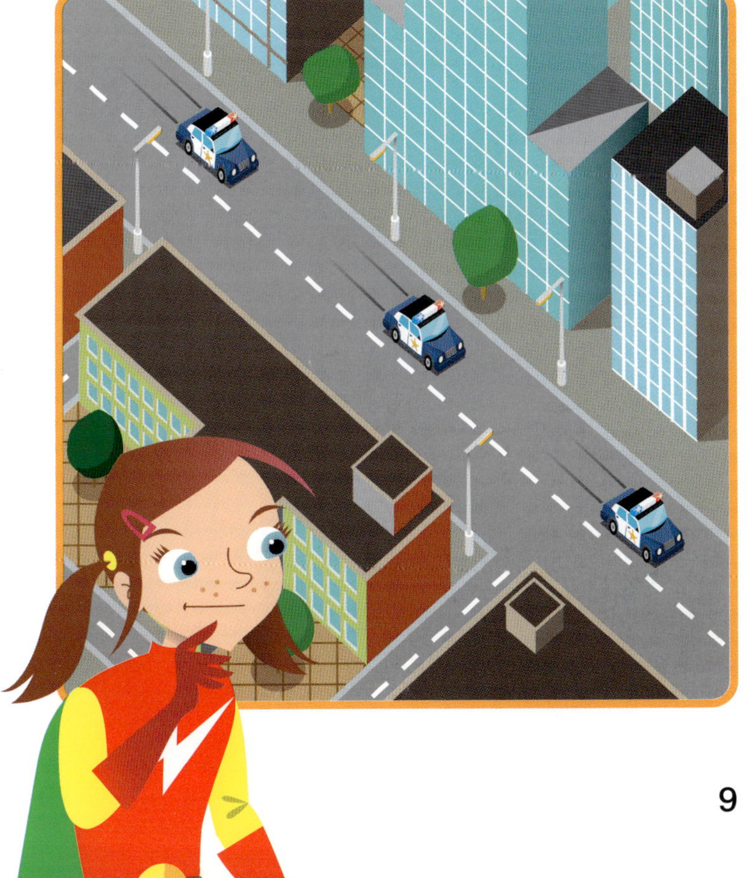

…the bank!

"A robber must be robbing the bank!" says Jade.

She hides behind a chimney
to see. Police cars screech all
around the bank.

Jade can see from behind the chimney.

Just then, a hatch opens on the roof of the bank. Jade can see a hand. Out gets…

…Dax Doom!

"Look!" gasps Jumping Jade,
"he has a big sack of gold!"

Jumping Jade can see Dax Doom strapping on...

...a flying machine!

As Jade looks on, Dax Doom
checks his straps. With a sneaky
grin, he presses a button.
The wings start to spin.

Just as the police get onto the roof, off zooms Dax Doom.

They see Dax Doom zoom away.
"Oh, no!" puff the police.
"We have lost him!"

"Not so fast," says Jade. When
Dax Doom flies near, she jumps!

Jade grabs Dax Doom and pulls

him back down to the roof of…

21

...the jail! The police run all the way down the stairs of the bank.

They run all the way down
the street.

22

They run all the way up the stairs
and onto the roof of the jail.

23

"Good work, Jade!" puff the police.
Dax Doom is in handcuffs.

"Let me go!" he shouts as they take him down the stairs into the jail.

"Thanks, Jade," say the police.
"You helped us to catch
Dax Doom."

And now Dax Doom is safely
behind bars.
Or is he?

Superhero Secret Puzzles

- ★ What is Jade's superpower?

- ★ How does Jade know there is a bank-robber?

- ★ What does Jade hide behind?

- ★ How does Dax Doom get away from the police?

- ★ What is in Dax Doom's sack?

- ★ Where does Jade take Dax Doom?

- ★ How high can you jump?

Look at these pictures from the story and say the order they should go in.

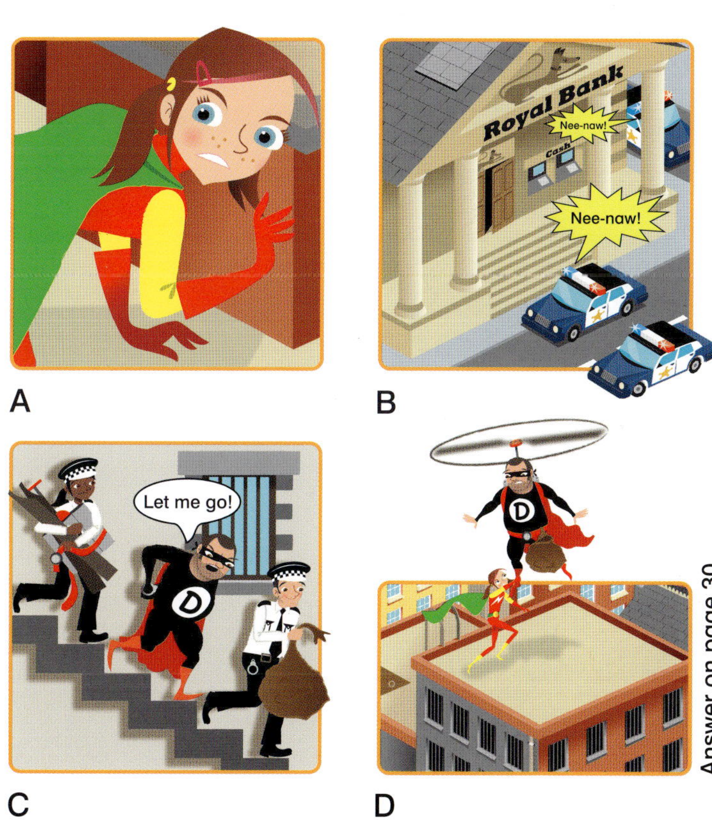

A

B

C

D

Tricky Words Memory Quiz

Can you remember these
words from the story?

See if you can read them super-fast.

to	the	they	so	you
do	be	oh	work	
one	all	no	me	
when	out	we	go	
she	he	have	into	

What else can you remember?

Can you put the book down and say
what happens in the story?